X BIOGRAPHY
W112.5
KEITH, TED
Dwyane Wade.

WITHDRAWN

D1540608

DwyaneWADE

By Ted Keith

ST. CHARLES PARISH LIBRARY
105 LAKEWOOD DRIVE
P.O. BOX 949
LULING, LA 70070

WITHDRAWN

The
Child's
World®
www.childsworld.com

Published in the United States of America by The Child's World®
1980 Lookout Drive • Mankato, MN 56003-1705
800-599-READ • www.childsworld.com

ACKNOWLEDGMENTS

The Child's World®: Mary Berendes, Publishing Director

Produced by Shoreline Publishing Group LLC
President / Editorial Director: James Buckley, Jr.
Designer: Tom Carling, carlingdesign.com
Assistant Editor: Jim Gigliotti

Photo Credits: Cover: Corbis.
All interior photos AP/Wide World except Corbis: 1, 3, 22.

Copyright © 2008 by The Child's World®
All rights reserved. No part of this book may be reproduced or utilized in any form or by any means without written permission from the publisher.

LIBRARY OF CONGRESS
CATALOGING-IN-PUBLICATION DATA

Keith, Ted.
  Dwyane Wade / by Ted Keith.
      p. cm. — (The world's greatest athletes)
  Includes index.
  ISBN 978-1-59296-880-0 (library bound : alk. paper)
 1. Wade, Dwyane, 1982– 2. Basketball players—United States—Biography. I. Title. II. Series.

  GV884.W36K45 2008
  796.323092—dc22
  [B]

                                        2007032000

CONTENTS

Making Things Happen

IT WAS GAME 5 OF THE 2006 NATIONAL BASKETBALL Association (NBA) Finals. There were fewer than 10 seconds left on the clock in overtime. The Miami Heat were down by one point...and Dwyane Wade had the ball. It was the moment Dwyane had waited years for—there was no way he was going to lose.

Dwyane knew exactly what to do. He would attack, just as he always does. He would ignore the physical pain that could come from a hard foul—or the emotional pain that could come from missing the shot—and go hard to the basket anyway. Because when your whole life has been about making something happen, that's what you do when the moment is biggest. Sure enough, Dwyane drew a foul. He made the two free throws that pushed the Heat in front of the Dallas Mavericks 101–100 with less than two seconds remaining. The free throws were the **capstone** to a brilliant play and a brilliant game by a brilliant player.

Never mind that the Mavericks threw four defenders—four!—at Dwyane in a futile effort to stop him. They could have thrown all 12 players on their roster, their coaches, even football's Dallas *Cowboys*—and Dwyane would have found a way to succeed. That is what he has been doing throughout his career.

Dwyane entered his fifth NBA season in 2007–08. He has emerged as the top **combo guard** in the league. He has the vision and passing skills of a point guard, and the athletic ability and size of a shooting guard. He is a game-changing force on offense and a tireless worker on defense. His combination of skill and will has turned the NBA into Wade's World.

Dwyane was clutch in the fifth game of the 2006 Finals against Dallas.

CHAPTER 1

Growing Up in Wade's World

DWYANE WADE WAS BORN ON JANUARY 17, 1982, in Chicago, Illinois. He was named after his father, Dwayne, but his birth certificate was misspelled Dwyane. His parents split up shortly after he was born. Dwyane's mother, Jolinda, was a drug and alcohol **addict**, so Dwyane's main parenting influence came from his sister Tragil, who is just five years older than he is.

In 1988, Tragil made a difficult decision. To keep her brother away from the drugs and gangs that had infested their neighborhood, she put him on a bus and told him they were going to the movies. Instead, she dropped him off at their father's house and left him there. At the time, Dwyane was hurt. He didn't realize what his sister was doing was for his own

Dwyane's road to the hardwood floors of professional basketball began on a concrete driveway in Illinois.

good. "It was two days before I realized she wasn't coming back," Dwyane told *USA Today* in 2005. "She was trying to get me away from the gangs and drugs . . . outside our mother's house, in our faces, every day. She didn't want me to get caught up in it."

A year later, Dwyane moved with his new family to a house in a **suburb** of Chicago. In the driveway

When Dwyane was honored at a Father of the Year event in 2007, his mom was there to share the moment.

of that house, Dwyane first began developing the basketball skills that would one day take him away from that dangerous life for good. Before he could be great at basketball, though, he had to learn to want to play. "At first I didn't like basketball," Dwyane said. "My father loved it, and he made me play. I used to like baseball and football. But he took me to the court and made me play for a week straight. I fell in love with the game. Then he didn't have to make me play, he had to stop me from playing."

In fact, Dwyane's father became his biggest competitor. His dad had been in the army for three years. He would make his son perform drills at all hours of the day and night. He reminded him that to be great, he had to work hard—and to be the best, he had to work harder than everybody else.

Dwayne and Dwyane played in hundreds of two-on-two games in the family driveway that were rough, foul-filled affairs. In the NBA, Dwyane has become known as a player who can drive to the basket without fear, often **absorbing** punishing contact while still being able to make the shot. It's a skill he developed while playing those rugged games with his dad and friends.

Dwyane was a national Father of the Year honoree in 2007. Among the sports stars honored in previous years was NBA great Patrick Ewing.

Young Dwyane Wade

> Because he didn't have to spend his summers traveling to the top basketball camps, Dwyane spent one summer working at a local KFC.

> Dwyane's mom spent time in jail and was addicted to drugs and alcohol. So Dwyane went to live with his father when he was eight years old.

> Dwyane started dating his future wife when he was a sophomore in high school.

> "There were no birthday presents or Christmas gifts," Dwayne told *USA Today* in 2005. "You just didn't ask for what you wanted. It was my mission as a young kid to overcome being poor. I had so many dreams, so many aspirations."

Basketball wasn't the only thing Dwyane discovered in his new environment, though. One of his new neighbors was a girl named Siohvaughn Funches. By the time Dwyane was a sophomore at Richlands High, they were dating. Two years later, while Siohvaughn was a freshman in college, Dwyane moved in with her mother while his father and stepmother endured marriage problems.

On the basketball court, Dwyane was quietly developing into an aggressive scorer, a strong passer, and a talented defender. He didn't make the varsity of his high school team until his junior season, though. That kept him from showing his skills at the big summer camps. At those camps, the top players are identified and scouted. They often receive scholarship offers from the country's best basketball schools. Dwyane's academic work wasn't helping, either. He failed to qualify by one point on his ACT score, leaving his college future very much up in the air.

Coach Crean stood by Dwyane during his college career at Marquette.

Tom Crean saw potential in Dwyane—not only as a player, but also as a person. Tom was the head coach at Marquette University in Milwaukee, Wisconsin. Marquette was one of just three schools to recruit Dwyane. Tom convinced the admissions department to admit Dwyane in the fall of 2000 as a "partial qualifier." That meant he would be enrolled and allowed to practice with the team, but not be allowed to play in any games. He would lose that year of **eligibility**.

Just because Dwyane sat out, however, doesn't mean he sat around. Crean put Dwyane to work in practice helping develop the other players. The coach had him play as many positions as possible, which would eventually help Dwyane become the **multi-faceted** star he is now. Crean also had Dwyane take note of the way teams played in games. At halftime, Dwyane would tell his teammates what they had done right and what they needed to do better.

Dwyane finally got on the court as a sophomore in 2001–02, putting his pointers, and his points, to good use. He led the team in virtually every important category: scoring (17.8 points per game), rebounds (6.6 per game), assists (3.4), steals (2.5), and blocks (1.1). As a junior, he was even better. He was named a first-team All-America as well as the Conference USA Player of the Year.

That was enough to return Marquette basketball to **prominence** and make Dwyane a star. But when the NCAA Tournament came, Dwyane was even better. In the Midwest Regional Final against a top-seeded and top-ranked Kentucky team that had

Marquette had not played in college basketball's Final Four since 1977 until Dwyane led the Golden Eagles there in 2003.

Dwyane's number 3 was retired by Marquette in 2007. You can see him talking at the ceremony in the reflection on the glass.

won 26 straight games, Dwyane put on one of the great performances in college basketball history. He had a **triple-double**—29 points, 11 rebounds, and 11 assists—and Marquette cruised to an 83-69 win.

Though Marquette went on to lose in the national semifinals to Kansas, Dwyane had established himself as an NBA-level talent. He declared himself eligible for the NBA draft.

Commissioner David Stern (left) welcomed Dwyane to the NBA after Miami chose him with the fifth pick in the 2003 draft.

CHAPTER 2

Dwyane Heats Up

THE 2003 NBA DRAFT WAS EXPECTED TO BE A special one even before Dwyane entered his name. High school **phenom** LeBron James finally was eligible to be drafted, as well as college star Carmelo Anthony, who had just led Syracuse to the national championship. Along with international teenage sensation Darko Milicic, there seemed to be several franchise players available.

As it turned out, though, Dwyane would lead his team to an NBA title before any of them. Of course, the Miami Heat didn't know that when they selected Dwyane with the fifth overall choice. But Heat coach Pat Riley sensed his team had made a big addition when he spoke about Dwyane that night. "He was probably the most **mature** player we worked out and scouted," Pat said. "Not only do I see him as a multiple-position player, but I also see him as a guy who can defend. Not only can he defend, but he's also a defensive player who can score and rebound. He's an absolutely complete player who can get better. We are absolutely excited with this pick."

Dwyane entered the league without any of the fanfare of James or Anthony, and it bothered him. "It was like, move out of the way, Dwyane, let Carmelo and LeBron take a picture," he told *Sports Illustrated* in 2006. "I felt slighted. I thought, 'I can be on these guys' level, so what am I going to do to get there?'"

Not everyone overlooked him, though. One teammate, Eddie Jones, called Dwyane the best rookie in the league during training camp before the season even started. Dwyane brushed it off, but Jones wasn't the only teammate who took note of the rookie's skills.

"You meet guards in this league who are too small to play shooting guard so they have to play point guard," then-Heat forward Lamar Odom told the *Miami Herald*. "It's not like that with Dwyane. He's 6-4, but he's strong. He's got long arms and he's got a point guard's IQ."

Dwyane was a shooting guard most of his life, but he became the starting point guard for the Heat during his rookie season of 2003-04.

Dwyane didn't back down from anybpdy during his rookie season. He was an impact player from the start.

Dwyane soon set about showing the rest of the NBA that his teammates were correct to praise him so much. With Riley having stepped down as coach just before the season started, Dwyane and the rest of the Heat were thrown off track. Nevertheless, Dwyane put together a **stellar** rookie year. Although

Dwyane's Big Moment

When Dwyane Wade arrived at Marquette, he was a relatively unknown player from Chicago who had been recruited by just three schools. While sitting out as a freshman because of his grades, he spent hours practicing, but not playing with his team. "When we lost, Coach Crean was harder on me than anybody else," Dwyane remembers. "He'd blame me and say it was my fault because I hadn't practiced hard enough."

Two years later, though, Dwyane was often the reason the Golden Eagles were winning. He was a first-team All-America, but people still doubted whether he was a great player—someone who could succeed in the NBA. But in the biggest game of his life, Dwyane did something only two other players had ever done: He posted a triple-double in an NCAA Tournament game. He had 29 points, 11 rebounds, and 11 assists against the top-ranked team in the country, the Kentucky Wildcats. Dwyane's performance lifted Marquette to a victory that propelled the school to the Final Four.

"We just couldn't contain his talent," said Kentucky guard Keith Bogans.

he missed 21 games with injury, he still managed to average 16.2 points per game and finish third in the Rookie of the Year balloting behind only James and Anthony. He showed enough ability that he was selected to play for Team USA at the 2004 Summer Olympics in Athens, Greece.

Dwyane was a surprising choice. (He was so unknown even among his teammates that U.S. forward Tim Duncan of the San Antonio Spurs said he didn't know Dwyane could play point guard, mistaking him for a wing player.) But he gained valuable experience playing with, and against, the best players in the world.

"He's special," coach Larry Brown told the *Milwaukee Journal-Sentinel*. "There's not an area that he does not excel in, and there's not a possession that goes by that he doesn't want to get better."

The United States finished with a disappointing bronze medal in the Olympics. It was the first time the United States failed to capture gold with NBA players on the roster. That was news. But there was even bigger news in the NBA that summer. Dwyane was getting a new teammate on the Heat: center Shaquille O'Neal.

CHAPTER 3

Flash Forward to Stardom

SHAQUILLE O'NEAL, THE HULKING 7-1, 325-POUND center, came to Miami looking to add to his Hall of Fame résumé. The former MVP had led the Los Angeles Lakers to three NBA titles earlier in the 2000s, but he was getting older and was not as dominant as he had been. Still, the Heat didn't hesitate to grab O'Neal when the Lakers made him available. The pairing of Dwyane and Shaq instantly transformed the Heat into title contenders. After going 42-40 in Dwyane's rookie season, the Heat finished with the best record in the Eastern Conference in 2004–05, going 59–23.

To the casual observer, it may have seemed like this was another Shaq-led effort. Even Shaq, though, acknowledged that it was Dwyane who was leading

When massive center Shaquille O'Neal (32) joined Dwyane in Miami, the Heat were on their way to an NBA title.

Miami. Before the season began, Shaq sat down with the young star to tell him that it was Dwyane's team, and that he would be happy as the sidekick. Shaq even gave Dwyane a new nickname: Flash. It was after the comic-book superhero, and it was a reference to Dwyane's speed and quickness.

Not that Shaq was completely ready to get out of the way. Once, in practice, Dwyane tried to dunk on his new center, only to be sent to the ground with a hard foul. "He told me, 'Never try that again,'" Dwyane said. "He put me down on the ground. I never tried again."

Dwyane didn't mind trying against everyone else, though. He was quickly developing a reputation as a player unafraid of contact. His frequent trips into the lane often ended up with him taking a hard hit.

Dwyane (wearing number 9) and fellow superstar Carmelo Anthony played on the U.S. National Team in 2006.

But they also often wound up with him at the free throw line, where he could help his team. That year, Dwyane led the team in free throws made on his way to a club-record 24.1 points per game. "He attacks, attacks, attacks," Minnesota Timberwolves guard Sam Cassell told *Sports Illustrated* in 2005. "There are a lot of guys in this league who can get to the rim, but Dwyane has the strength to finish," added then-Charlotte Bobcats coach Bernie Bickerstaff.

Dwyane was also developing into the best combo guard in the league. Everyone always knew about his scoring ability. But Elton Brand, who played with Wade on the U.S. National Team, noted that Dwyane also is a top-notch passer. "His passing skill is what really surprised me," Brand said. "All I had to do was drop the ball in the basket."

In addition to playing in his first NBA All-Star Game in February of 2005, Dwyane also was named second team All-NBA and second-team All-Defense that season.

"I knew Flash was good," an impressed Shaq told *Sports Illustrated*. "He's just gooder than I thought."

Dwyane was at his "goodest" during the playoffs when he helped the Heat to sweeps in the first two

In the 2006 NBA All-Star Game, Dwyane scored 20 points. His basket with 16 seconds left broke a tie and gave the East a 122-120 victory.

rounds. But Dwyane got hurt during Game 7 of the Eastern Conference Finals, and that was enough to keep Miami from reaching the NBA Finals.

The next year, Dwyane wouldn't let anything keep him from a championship. During the 2005–06 regular season, he averaged 27.2 points, 5.7 rebounds, and 6.7 assists per game. The Heat won 52 games and earned the second seed in the Eastern Conference playoffs, but they drew a tough first round matchup against the Chicago Bulls. In Game 5, with the series tied at two wins apiece, Dwyane suffered a hip injury and missed more than eight minutes of game action. He returned with the Bulls leading by five points. Right after Flash came back, he led the Heat on a 7-0 run to regain the lead—and control of the series. The Heat won that game and the next to advance to the next round against the New Jersey Nets.

Once again, Dwyane played the hero. He stole the inbounds pass on the last play of the Heat's series-clinching victory in Game 5. It prevented the Nets from attempting a game-winning shot that might have swung momentum back to them. Instead, the Heat headed to the conference finals and a rematch against the Pistons.

Jason Kidd (5) and the Nets did their best, but they couldn't stop Dwyane and the Heat during the 2006 playoffs.

Miami won three of the first four games against the Pistons. But during a Game 5 loss in Detroit, Dwyane began feeling ill. Two days later, he was up all night vomiting. He checked himself into the hospital with what turned out to be a stomach virus. Dwyane left the hospital that afternoon and drove to American Airlines Arena in Miami for Game 6. Although still sick and **dehydrated**, Dwyane willed himself to a double-double with 14 points and 10 assists, helping the Heat to a series-clinching, 95–78 win.

In the Finals, the Dallas Mavericks won the first two games. Then, they were ahead in Game 3 by 13 points with just six-and-a-half minutes to play. Dwyane led a frantic charge that helped Miami pull out a 98–96 win. He finished with 42 points and 13 rebounds, and again clinched the victory by stealing an inbounds pass on the last play.

Dwyane was named the most valuable player of Miami's win in the '06 Finals.

The next three games belonged to Dwyane. In the best Finals performance since the great Michael Jordan's **heyday** in the 1990s, Dwyane overwhelmed the Mavericks. He scored 36, then 43, then 36 points as the Heat won all three games to win their first NBA title.

In His Own Words

Dwyane told *Sports Illustrated* in 2006:

▶ *"Anybody can be great in life when things are going good. What about when things are going bad? It's bad moments that make a person. You're going to fall. It's how you get up that defines you as a man."*

In *USA Today* in 2005, Dwyane said:

▶ *"I'm living the life I imagined. I'm playing in the NBA. I'm playing on one of the best teams. I'm playing in one of the best cities. People know me around the world. I've got the family I want. Everything I wanted, I got, and I'm happy."*

Although a severe shoulder injury hampered Dwyane and kept the Heat from repeating as champions in 2007, he had firmly established himself as a star of the highest order.

Still, it did not change Dwyane's humble nature. When he appeared at Disney World after winning the Finals MVP award, he bused hundreds of children from inner-city and underprivileged homes to celebrate with him. It was just the latest example of Dwyane's kindness and generosity. He is a loving father to his wife and their sons Zaire and Zion.

Dwyane's wife? She is Siohvaughn, the same girl he met when he was eight years old and has dated since he was 15. In 2007, Dwyane was honored as a National Father of the Year. And even though he was hurt and couldn't play basketball for most of the second half of the season, he didn't stop being a good person. In April of 2007, he threw a surprise party for 75 patients at the Miami Children's Hospital.

Even Dwyane's mom is doing better. After spending time in jail, she kicked her addictions and is now an ordained pastor at a Baptist church. Dwyane, who gives 10 percent of his income to his church, helped carry his mom through her darkest hours. He is able to help her, and the rest of his family, share in his success.

"There's an awe about Dwyane, not only in his game but in his whole approach to life," Heat coach Pat Riley once said to USA Today. "His sincerity, his humility. All of those things are strength when it comes to greatness."

In a career that has already been marked by success in overcoming obstacles and bouncing back from disappointment, there can be little doubt that Dwyane Wade is destined for greatness.

Dwyane Wade's Career Statistics

BORN: January 17, 1982   **BIRTHPLACE:** Chicago, Illinois

HEIGHT: 6-4   **WEIGHT:** 216

DRAFTED: First round (fifth pick), 2003

Season	G-GS	MPG	FG%	3P%	FT%	RPG	APG	SPG	BPG	PPG
2003-04	61-56	34.9	46.5	30.2	74.7	4.1	4.5	1.4	0.6	16.3
2004-05	77-77	38.6	47.8	28.9	76.3	5.2	6.8	1.6	1.1	24.1
2005-06	75-75	38.6	49.5	17.1	78.3	5.7	6.7	2.0	0.8	27.2
2006-07	51-50	37.9	49.1	26.6	80.8	4.7	7.5	2.1	1.2	27.4
4 years	264-258	37.6	48.4	24.9	77.7	5.0	6.4	1.7	0.9	23.8

LEGEND: G-GS: games played–games started; MPG: minutes played per game; FG%: field-goal shooting percentage; 3P%: three-point shooting percentage; FT%: free-throw shooting percentage; RPG: rebounds per game; APG: assists per game; SPG: steals per game; BPG: blocked shots per game; PPG: points per game.

GLOSSARY

absorbing to take in or soak up

addict someone who has a bad habit that controls their actions

capstone the top achievement

combo guard neither a true point guard nor a shooting guard, the combo guard can perform the duties of both of those basketball positions

dehydrated a dangerous state of not having enough fluids in the body

eligibility qualified to play, according to certain rules

Final Four the semifinal and final rounds of the NCAA basketball championship playoffs

heyday the time of greatest success

mature able to act properly for one's age

multi-faceted able to do many different things or perform different roles

phenom a person who excels at a young age

prominence widely and favorably known

stellar excellent or outstanding

suburb a smaller town outside of a large city

triple-double reaching totals of 10 or more in three statistical categories (usually, but not always, points, rebounds, and assists)

FIND OUT MORE

BOOKS

Meet Dwyane Wade: Basketball's Rising Star
  By John Smithwick
  New York: PowerKids Press, 2007.
  A great biography of the Miami Heat superstar.

NBA Superstars 2006
  By Fiona Simpson
  New York: Scholastic Inc., 2006.
  This book features some of the NBA's brightest stars—
  including Dwyane Wade and Shaquille O'Neal.

The Story of the Miami Heat
  By Sara Gilbert
  Mankato, Minnesota: Creative Education, 2006.
  This book traces the club's history from its beginnings to the
  present era of Dwyane Wade.

WEB SITES

Visit our Web page for lots of links about Dwyane Wade:
www.childsworld.com/links

Note to Parents, Teachers, and Librarians: We routinely check our Web links to
make sure they're safe, active sites—so encourage your readers to check them out!

INDEX

ABOUT THE AUTHOR

Ted Keith is a senior writer for *Sports Illustrated for Kids*. He has covered many sports for the magazine and has also written books for kids on Kevin Garnett and on some NBA teams.